I know I Can!
Wrap a Gift

ANTHEA DAVIDSON-JARRETT
Illustrated by
Aldana Penayo
Published by EDUCATE THE GLOBE,
London, UK, 2022.

ISBN: 978-1-913804-06-0

Copyright © 2022 Educate The Globe Limited. All rights reserved. No part of this book is to be reprinted, copied or stored in retrieval systems of any type, except by written permission from the author. Part of this book may, however, be used only in reference to support related documents or subjects.

I know I can do it!

Please can I help?

I want to do it all by myself!

Please can I try?

Can you show me how?

I'm not too small,

I am ready right now!

It's my uncle's birthday

so I bought him a mug

that says 'The Best Uncle'

but I need to wrap it up.

My brother says he'll help me.

He's got the wrapping paper;

I have brought the scissors

so that we can wrap it later.

Now we have finished

having something to eat

it's time to wrap my uncle's gift.

I hope this is easy.

Roll out the wrapping paper.

Lay it smooth and flat

across the table like

when I'm rolling out a mat!

In the middle of the paper

place the mug in the box.

Plenty of paper all around

but not too much!

Just enough to wrap

the box all around.

We don't want the box to show.

It must be green and gold,

not brown!

Wrap one side of the paper

over the box

so one side is fully covered

from the bottom to the top.

I will hold the side down

so it doesn't escape.

Nasir cuts a short strip

of Cellotape then he tapes!

We wrap the other side of

the paper to the middle.

This is like a puzzle!

This is like a riddle!

Tuck in the left and right sides

of the paper sticking out.

Fold both sides inward

so they hug the box around.

Nasir tapes the sides

so they don't unravel.

He shows me how

to fold the ends into a triangle.

Fold the top and the bottom

down and up so they meet.

Wrapping gifts is tricky

but Nasir makes it easy!

He folds the triangle tips

inwards to make it neat.

Gosh! When wrapping gifts,

how many folds do you need?

Nasir cuts the tape

and I stick the sides down.

One more thing to do

before he heads into town.

We wrap the ribbon around

the bottom, top and sides.

I couldn't do it on my own

but I'm so happy that I tried!

Hey! I know how to tie a bow

I do it with my laces!

We did it! We wrapped a gift!

Smiles all over our faces!

www.ingramcontent.com/pod-product-compliance
Lightning Source LLC
Chambersburg PA
CBHW041244240426

43670CB00027B/2990